Teacher's Guide for

TIAGO, EXPLORER OF BRAZIL

by Alice Lockmiller

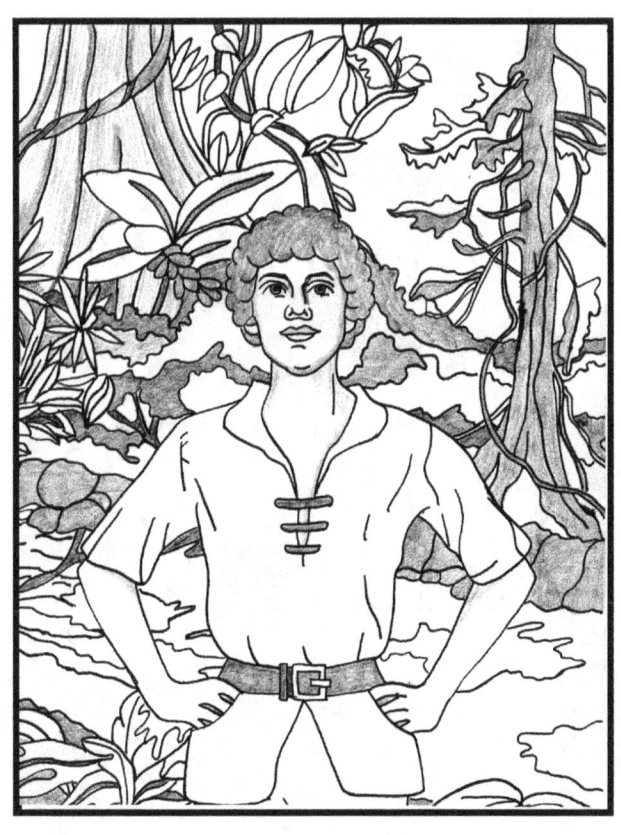

Printed in the United States of America

Layout and formatting by Charlotte Hamel

Illustrations by Alice Lockmiller

Published by www.lulu.com

ISBN: 978-0-557-36740-5

Table of Contents

Brazil

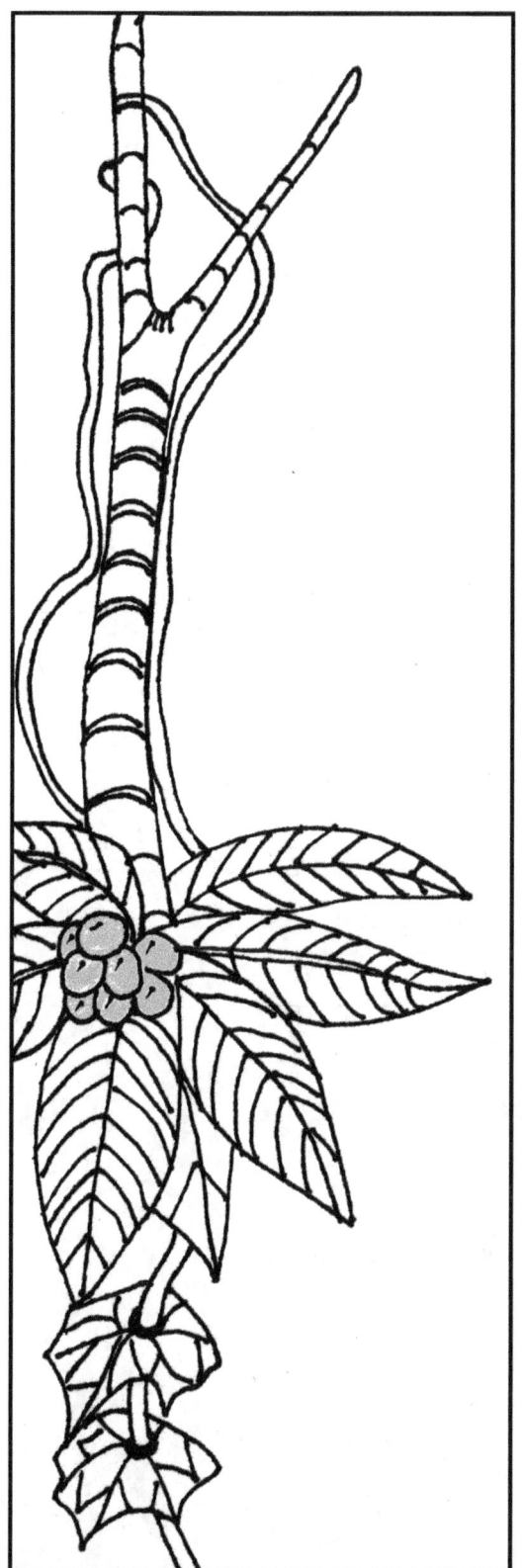

The country of Brazil lies in the southern hemisphere. It is the largest country in South America and fifth largest in the world. It shares borders with every other South American country except Equador and Chile.

The country is flat compared to its neighbors and is dominated by the world's largest river, the mighty Amazon, and its tributaries. The geography of Brazil includes plains, uplands, highland plateau, mountains, lakes, lagoons and many rivers.

The northern coastline has sand dunes and coastal tablelands. The Amazon region is home to the world's largest humid tropical rainforest.

The central plateau has small mountain ranges and large rivers. The plateau is divided into two areas of forest and woodland savanna (called cerrado).

The weather varies greatly in different parts of Brazil. The Amazon region is warm and humid. In the far south, the winters are cold. It snows in the central highlands, but coastal cities never get very cold. When it rains in Brazil, it is usually a short intense tropical downpour.

Brazil was colonized by Portugal. The official language is Portuguese, but many other languages are spoken there. In the the heart of the Amazon rainforest live tribes who have little or no contact with the outside world. Each tribe has its own language.

Map of South America

NAME _____ DATE _____

Using the map of South America and an atlas, write the name of each country beside the correct number below:

Argentina	Ecuador	Suriname
Bolivia	French Guiana	Uraguay
Brazil	Guayana	Venezuela
Chile	Paraguay	
Colombia`	Peru	

1. _____   8. _____

2. _____   9. _____

3. _____   10. _____

4. _____   11. _____

5. _____   12. _____

6. _____   13. _____

7. _____

Questions:

- Belém is located near the _____ degree latitude line.

- Brazil borders all other South American countries except _____ and _____.

- The Portuguese sailed across the _____ Ocean to Brazil.

South America

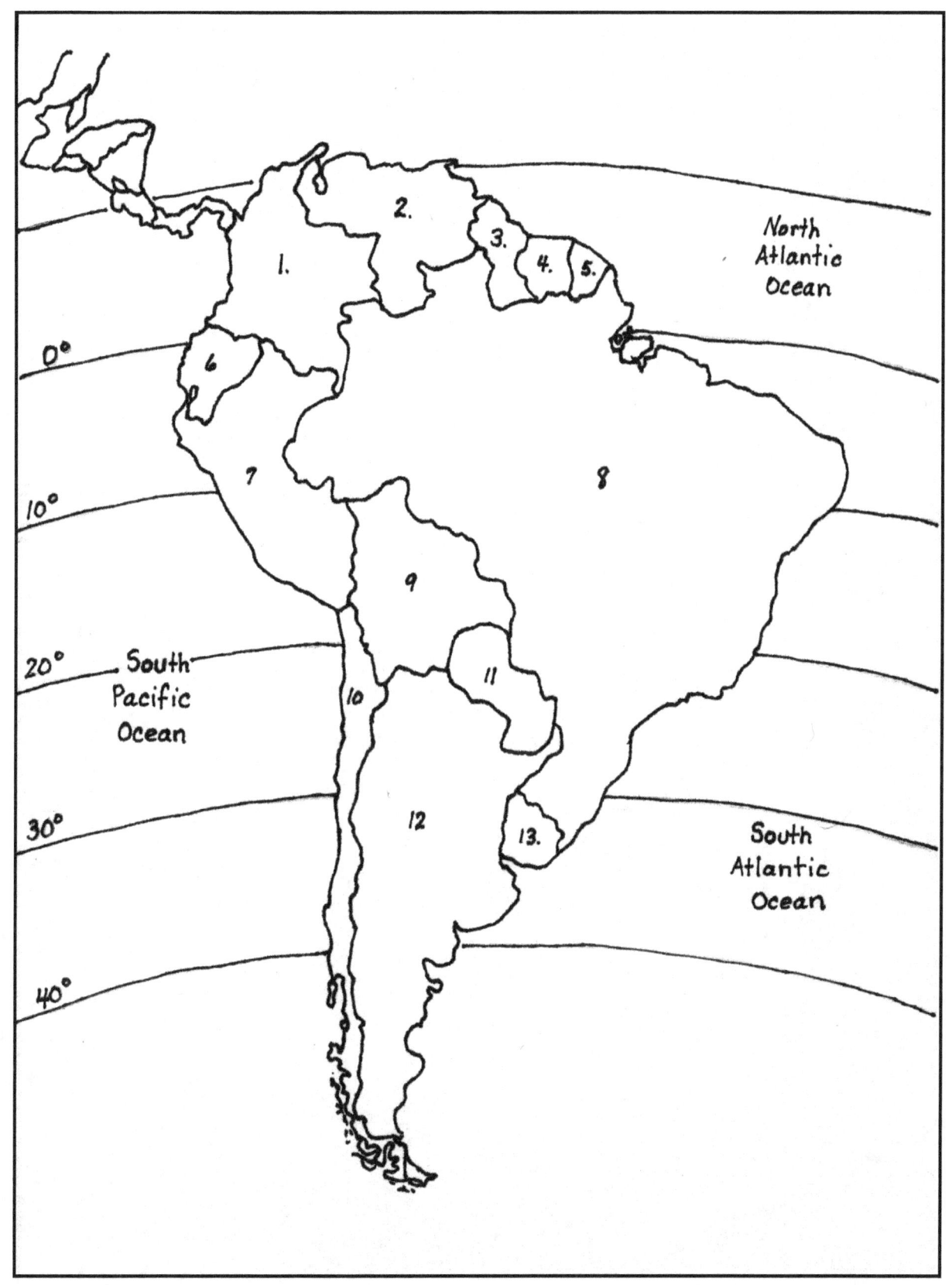

Portuguese Exploration

Portugal's long shoreline has many harbors and rivers flowing toward the Atlantic Ocean. It was a good environment for generations of adventurous seamen. They became leaders of exploration during the Middle Ages. The expeditions led to increased interest in nautical science, astronomy, navigation, and carotgraphy.

Until the 15th century, the Portuguese used small, fragile boats and could not explore the ocean. The ship that began discoveries along the African coast was called the caravel. The caravel was agile and easy to navigate. It had three masts but limited capacity for cargo and crew. Larger ships were also developed as merchant ships.

Prince Henry the Navigator provided Portual's ship captains with the best information, instruments, and maps that could be obtained. Voyages of discovery became highly profitable.

After the discovery of the West Indies by Christopher Columbus, the Spanish and Portuguese needed to determine areas they would explore.

Both Spain and Portual were Roman Catholic and the kings recognized the pope in Rome as their political and spiritual leader. In 1494, Pope Alexander VI authorized the Treaty of Tordesillas. It gave Portugal all the lands which might be discovered east of a straight line drawn from the Arctic Pole to the Antarctic. Spain received areas west of the line. This line was approximately at the 46° meridian (*crossing the equator NE of Belém*). Without the tools we have today, the countries debated over the placement for several years.

The treaty recognized Portugal's prestige in sailing and exploration. This prestige was improved when Vasco da Gama completed a voyage to India in 1497-1499.

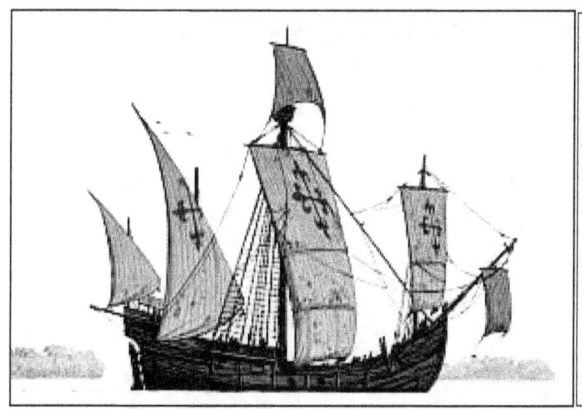
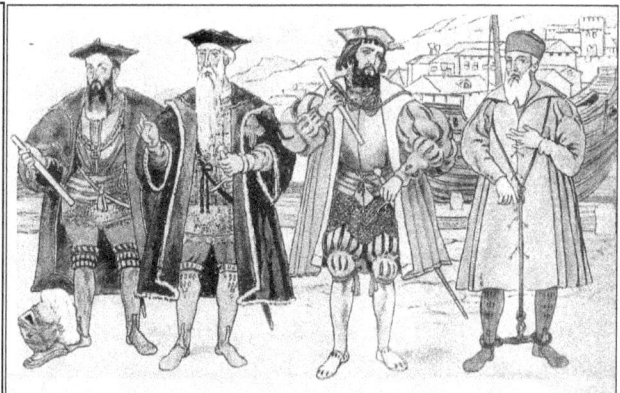

Colonial Brazil

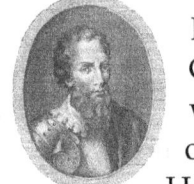 In 1500, Pedro Alvares Cabral discovered Brazil when his ship was blown off course on a trip to India. He stumbled on the southern coast of the current Brazilian state of Bahia. Sailing northward, he found a small harbor and named it Porto Seguro (*Safe Port*). The Portuguese planted a cross and claimed the land for King Manuel I. They believed it was an island and named it Vera Cruz (*True Cross*).

Two exiles were left there to learn the language and customs of the natives. One ship returned home with the report of the discovery, but the rest resumed the voyage to India. It was not an important discovery because no gold or precious stones were found.

Explorations confirmed it was not an island but an abundance of brazilwood was found for making red dye. In time, this brazilwood gave the new land its name. (*Not the nut species.*)

Thirteen ships and 1,000 men later landed in northeastern Brazil. European adventurers lived with the natives and continued to learn the language and culture of the local Tupi Indians. Colonial villages were built on the coast.

Brazil was divided into fifteen captaincies, parallel strips of land ruled by noblemen or commoners loyal to the Crown. They were responsible to populate, administer, Christianize and defend their domain. Only two of them, Sao Vicente and Permambuco, prospered. They grew sugar cane for their sugar mills.

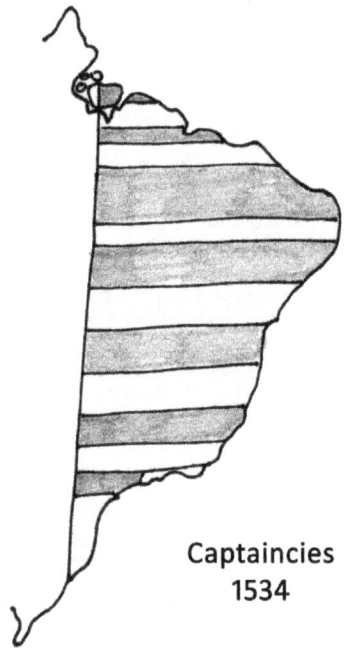

Captaincies 1534

Those who emigrated to Brazil were looking for land and an easy life. They had no intention of doing manual work and expected the native Indians to do the work for them. When the Indians refused to work for the colonists, the colonists made slaves of them. They took Indians captured in frequent wars between Indian Tribes or by taking people in raids on Indian villages.

Failing to enslave enough Tupi, the Portuguese began to ship African slaves to Brazil. These Africans had immunity to tropical diseases found in Brazil and were able workers in the tropical agriculture.

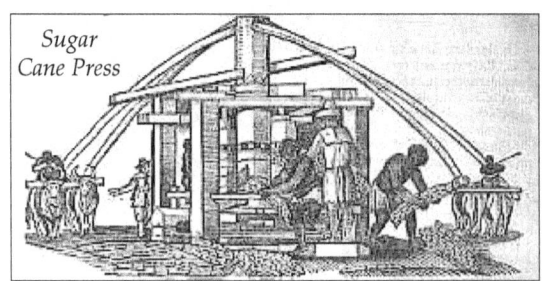

Sugar Cane Press

Continues

Colonial Brazil Continued.

The Portuguese justified their conquest of Brazil as spreading the Catholic faith. The Jesuits supported the king and extablished missions. They saved natives from slavery, studied native languages and converted the natives to Christianity.

The first capital of Brazil was Salvador da Bahia, founded in 1549. Salvador was the main slave port and the city's wealth was built on sugar and slavery of the sugar plantations. It was one of the most beautiful harbors in the world.

In 1616, a Portuguese fort was built at Belém in the captaincy (state) of Para. It became a busy port and an entrance gate to the Amazon. It was the first European colony on the Amazon and became an important port for sugar trade. However, the location of the settlement violated the treaty because it was on the Spanish side of the line.

In the book Tiago, Explorer of Brazil, the port settlement of Belém is Tiago's home, and a small group of Spanish soldiers and Franciscan monks arrived there. They had traveled down the Amazon. Inspired by their description of docile Indian tribes up the river, Portuguese Captain Pedro Teixeira led seventy soldiers and 1,100 Indians up the river in 1638. After eight months, the expedition made it to Quito, Equador, where they were held by Spanish authorities.

The Portuguese explorers were not clean people like the natives they found in Brazil. They brought diseases that killed hundreds or even thousands of natives.

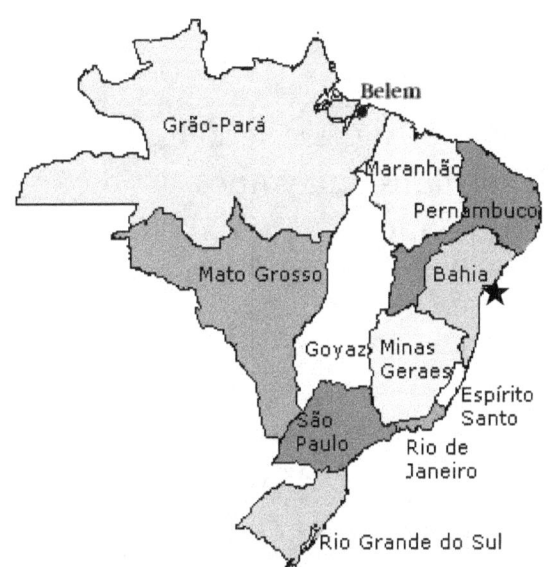

Brazil States 1787
★ First capital, Salvador
(1549 – 1763)

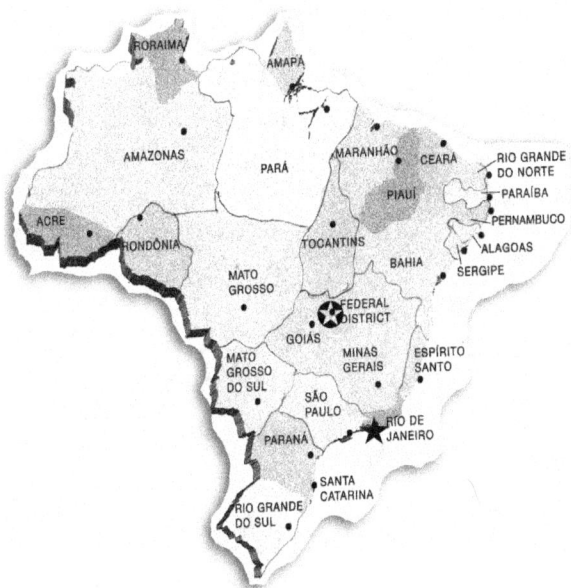

Brazil States Today
★ Capital, Rio de Janerio
(1763-1815)
✪ Current Capital, Brasilia

Settlers and Indians

The Portuguese settlers and the native Indians have different beliefs, traditions and values. Compare these two groups using the following chart. (*You could try it twice, before and after you read the article later on the Indians.*)

Some describing words you could use:

Indian Men	Portuguese Men
"Noble savages"	Bearded
Innocent	Hairy
Child of nature	Smelly
Hospitable	Base
Exotic	Brutal
Handsome	Practical
Unsophisticated	Experienced
Clean	Worked for profit
Painted bodies	Expected glory
Warriors	Sought riches
Coppery skin	Wore hats and boots
Hunters	Slovenly
Fishermen	Diseased
Craftsmen	Sailors
Cannibals	New crusaders
Enjoyed life	Life is a chore
Believed in spirits and animism	Believed in God
Naked	Exile

Comparison Chart

NAME: _____ DATE _____

	Settlers	**Indians**
Attitude toward cleanliness		
Attitude toward religion		
Household responsibilities		
Social life		
Attitude toward family		
Family influences on her/his life		

Amazon River

Tens of thousands of streams feed the muddy Amazon River, the largest river in the world. It pours 170 billion gallons of water into the Atlantic Ocean every <u>hour</u>. At its lower reaches, the river is so broad that it is impossible to see from one side to the other. During the wet season, parts of the Amazon exceed 130 miles in width. The river is more than 4,000 miles long, second only in length to the Nile River in Egypt.

The river was named for the tribe of women warriors in Greek mythology called the "Amazons". The first European to explore it was the Spaniard Francisco de Orellana. He traveled almost the length of the river in 1541-1542 with his crew. On the way, they were attacked by female warriors and he called them Amazons.

The river begins its long journey high in the Andes Mountains of Peru. As it flows through Brazil, it gathers waters from over a thousand tributaries that do not have mouths on the sea. These include the Putumayo, Negro, Xinga and Trombetas.

The tributaries are referred to as either black or white. "Black" rivers like the Negro have acid formed from rocks and decomposing material from the florest floor. Black water (really the color red) contains few nutrients and animals cannot live there. The "white" water flows from the Andes and is melted snow and rain. It is full of animal life. At one point, the two colors flow separately along the same stretch of river. Parts of the Amazon river are olive green and similar to "black" rivers.

The river floods regularly in the upper part and once a year farther downstream. Much of the Amazon forest floor floods to depths of 30 feet for months. Some parts are under water most of the time. The Amazon basin averages 100 inches of rainfall each year. It is always hot, wet and sticky there.

Most of the river flows through tropical rainforest where there are few roads or cities. The average depth of the river during the height of the rainy season is 130 feet.

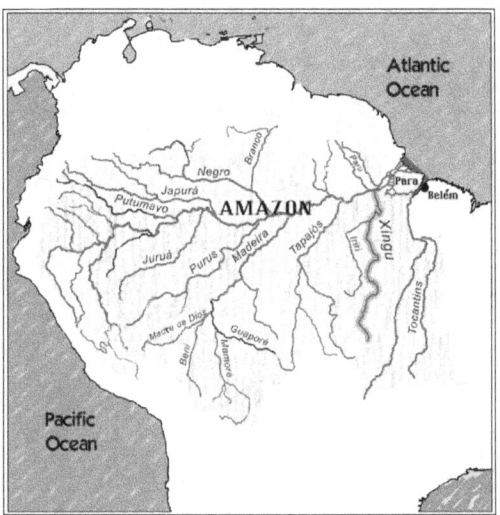

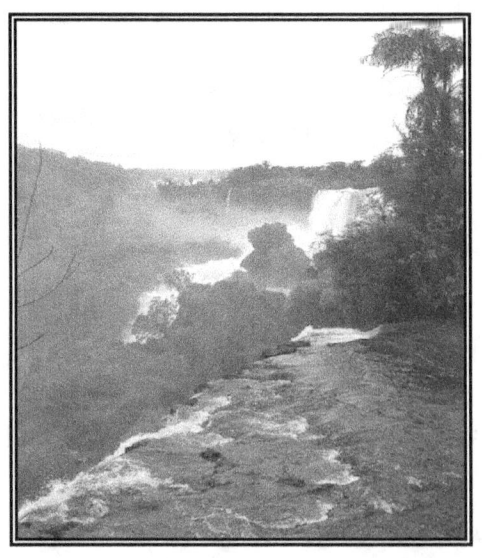

Amazon Rainforest

More than one-third of all species in the world live in the Amazon Rainforest.

It is the giant and rich tropical forest and river basin that covers over 2,100,000 square miles – over one-third of the country. The rainforest is the lowland type. Ninety percent of it is not flooded in the rainy season.

The rainforest is a unique ecosystem with several layers of plants and the animals that depend on these plants for survival. Tall trees provide dappled sunlight for smaller trees. The trunks of these trees support vines and creepers. The plants provide just the right humidity.

Birds and animals of the rainforest pollinate plants and spread seeds. Plants provide shelter and food for these birds and animals. Insects break down waste on the forest floor which creates compost to feed the plants.

The rainforest is also strange, uninviting and hostile. It is too dense and vast to be easily explored and there are many legends about the vicious and venomous creatures. The forest is always talking. A chorus of calls and other sounds fill the humid air.

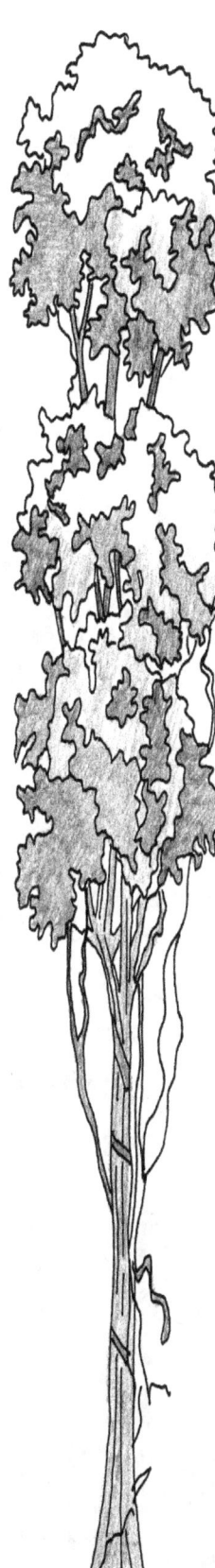

Rivers flow where trees grow close together and form a canopy blocking out the sun to everything below. Numerous plants thrive in the canopy including brightly colored orchids and emerald-green mosses and ferns.

Closer to the ground are more young trees, smaller trees and shrubs. The forest floor supports little vegetation. The forest is home to 20% of the world's plant and bird species and an immeasurable number of insects. There are 50,000 species of tropical plants and trees and half of them are only found in the Amazon region.

The plants are important to man as well. They give us Brazil nuts, rubber, pineapples and cocoa. The trees are prized for their mahogany, cedar and rosewood. Plants harvested for medicine include quinine, cocaine and curare. Rainforest plants are the basis for many modern medicines. Other plants produce dyes, flavorings and perfumes.

The Amazon is humid year-round with an average temperature of 80°F. The unique ecosystem supports 2,000 species of fish, 1,800 species of butterfly and over 200 species of mosquito. Thousands of colorful birds such as the toucan, parrot and macaw fly beneath the canopy.

An Explorer Named Fawcett

The mighty Amazon River of South America has been the scene of dangerous and fantastic adventures. Expeditions have spanned centuries and included conquistadors, adventurers and fortune hunters. Some explorers never expected to discover or travel down the Amazon and others sought this majestic river and its many tributaries for the secrets they held.

Francisco de Orellana was the first man from Europe known to travel down the Amazon, but he did not write about his travels. His expedition did little to encourage future ventures into this land of hostile Indians and constant hunger. Most believed an explorer in this land could only survive with God's help.

But one man's expeditions here have inspired legends, research and numerous explorers seeking to solve a mystery. This man was <u>Colonel Percy Harrison Fawcett.</u>

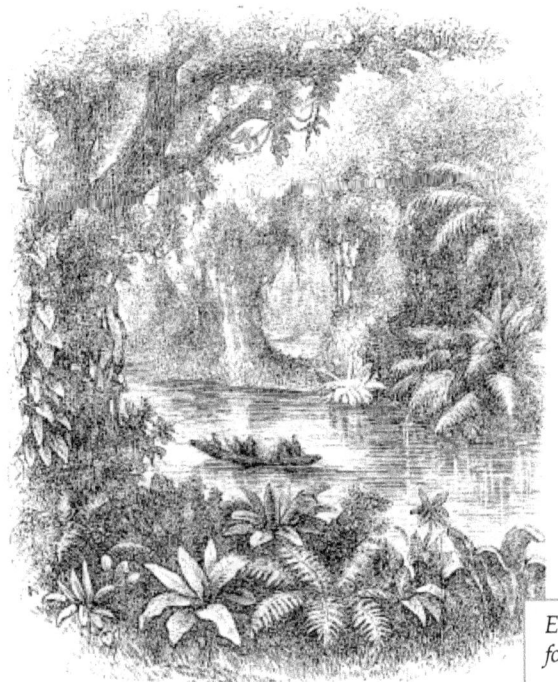

Col. Fawcett was born in England in 1867 and became a British archaeologist and explorer. He charted the wilderness of South America and in 1925, disappeared there without a trace. He was searching for an ancient lost city in the uncharted rainforest deep in the center of Brazil.

Colonel Fawcett made seven expeditions to South America between 1906 and 1924 to study local wildlife and archaeology. He had studied ancient legends and historical records and was convinced a lost city existed in the forest. He believed it was in the Mato Grosso region and called the city "Z".

Fawcett knew his expeditions were dangerous. He left instructions that no rescue expedition be sent if he did not return. Many presumed the local Indians killed him, but there is no proof he was murdered.

Fawcett, his son Jack and Jack's friend were reported to be exploring the Upper Xingu River, a tributary of the Amazon. The Kalapalo Indians were the last to see them alive and reported that the two younger men were ill. It is possible they all died of disease, like malaria, carried by the mosquitoes. Keep in mind that there were no antibiotics or other medicines to treat various illnesses.

Etchings in article from public domain found on www.gutenberg.org

Continues.

More than thirteen expeditions were sent to discover the fate of Colonel Fawcett and his small party. In 2005, a writer/reporter named David Grann visited the Kalapalo tribe. These Indians had an oral history about the explorers who had once stayed in their village. The Kalapalo had warned Fawcett not to go in the direction he'd chosen. They watched his campfire finally disappear in the land occupied by fierce Indians.

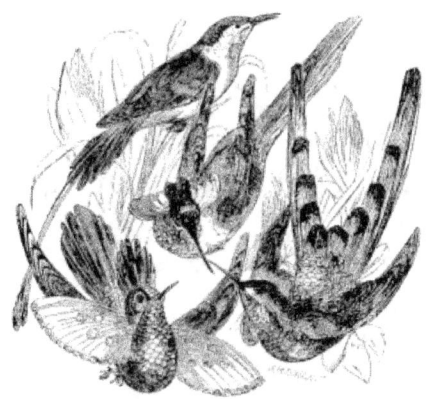

Brazilian Hummers

Since the disappearance of Fawcett, archaeologists have discovered that a monumental civilization may actually have existed near where he was looking. Archaeologist Michael Heckenberger and others have found evidence of the circular plazas, roads, holes for palisade walls and the ditches surrounding the large settlements.

Since the Indians had limited access to stone, their settlements were built of wood and other plant resources. When these settlements were abandoned, the forest buried or destroyed much of the evidence of these sites. Material from one site dates to A.D. 1283.

Colonel Fawcett was believed to be an inspiration for the character, "Indiana Jones". Fawcett's younger son, Brian, wrote an adventurous "autobiography" of his father using some of his notes. In Exploration Fawcett, Brian carefully omitted most of the facts.

David Grann recently uncovered this crucial material and wrote about it in The Lost City of Z. The reporter's book reveals details of Fawcett's life and evidence about the outcome of his fatal expedition.

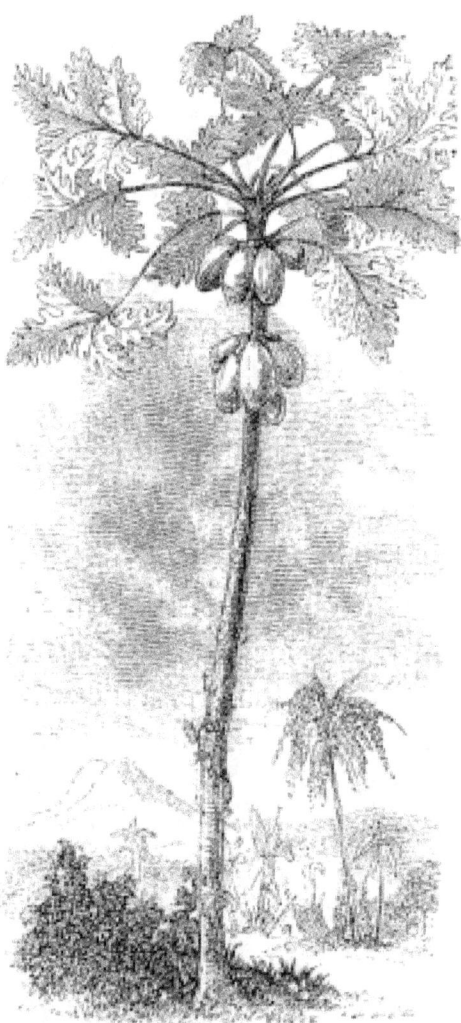

Papaya Tree

My Explorer Plan

NAME: _____ DATE: _____

    DIRECTIONS: You will follow the route Tiago and his family took to the Kalapalo village.   You may choose one traveling companion. Complete the planning sheet for your trip. Be sure your pack is not too heavy!

===

My partner is _____. I chose him/her

because _____.

FOOD:

Item	Reason

I will need _____

_____ to prepare food.

Continues.

Clothing:

Item	Reason

Other:

Item	Reason

Xingu River

In <u>Tiago, Explorer of Brazil</u>, the family travels on or near the Xingu River. Since it runs northward, they are traveling against the current.

The Xingu (*Shin-goo*) River is a 1,300-mile long river in northeast Brazil. It is one of the largest tributaries of the Amazon River. Three streams form the Xingu. The river is known for its succession of rapids that stretch over 400 miles. It is two and one-half miles wide at its mouth. The channel is deep where the waters mingle with those of the Amazon.

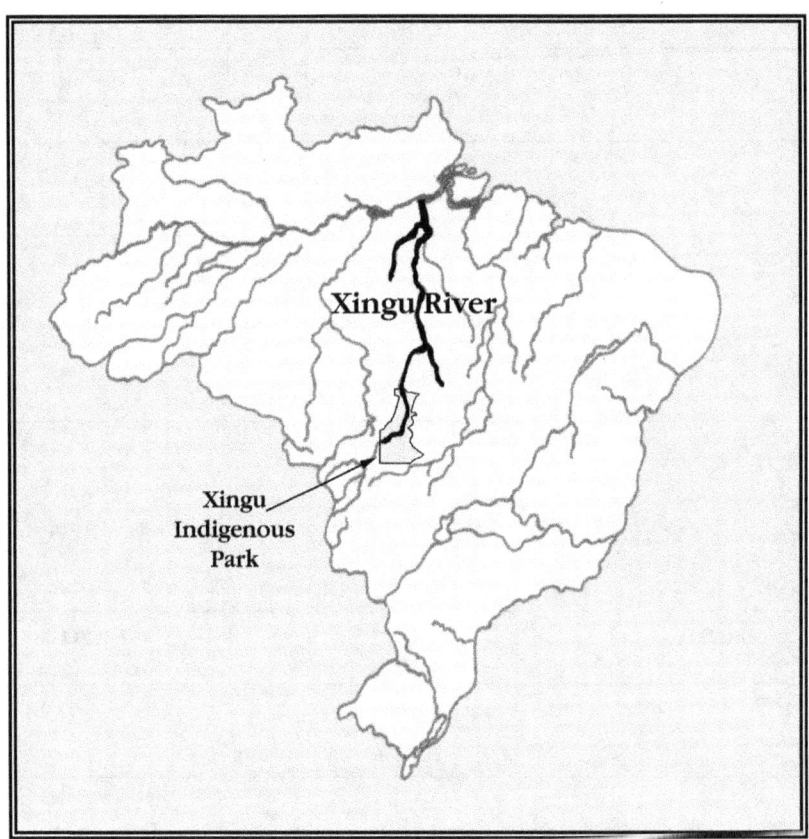

The channels of the Xingu River are difficult to navigate. The waters are healthy, clean and full of fish. The river flows over a rocky riverbed. The land around the river is flooded each year and rich sediment is left to grow a multitude of plants. The land is a place of wild but often hostile beauty.

There is now a large Indian park along the Xingu River and fourteen tribes of Indians live there. Like their ancestors, Brazilian Indians use the river for food and water. Their lifestyle and survival are in great danger. These lands and the river are threatened by uncontrolled forest exploration and farming around the park.

The Indians of the Xingu

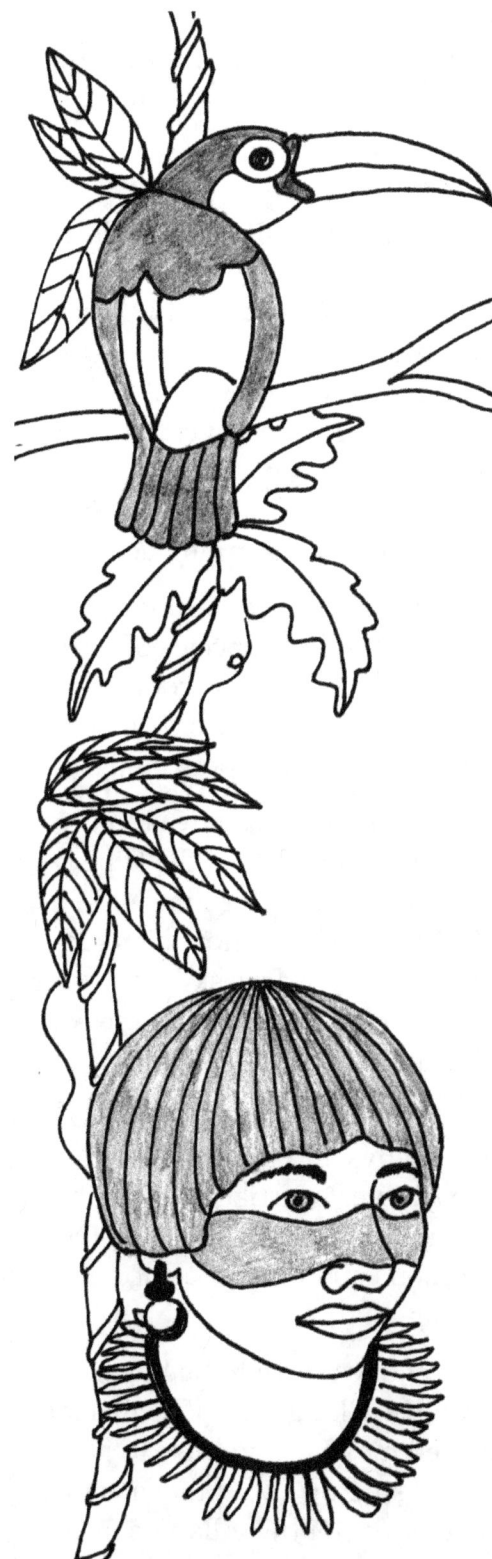

In the Xingu River Basin of the Amazon rainforest of Brazil live fifteen tribes of Indians. The tribes resemble one large nation because of their close relationships. These groups are small and they chose this area as a refuge and sought to maintain their cultural integrity.

There are two main concentrations of Indians in the Xingu area. One group is located near the upper river (i.e. south end) and one is about halfway down. The Kalapalo and Kiukuro are two of the Upper Xingu tribes.

But about 1200-1600 A.D., the native Amazonian people of the Upper Xingu transformed the landscape into large complex settlements. These were densely populated and included large agricultural areas, circular plazas with palisade walls and radial roads. There is evidence of moats, raised roads (i.e. for flooding) and bridges in and around these sites.

After about 1600-1700 A.D., catastrophic depopulation led to abandonment of these "cities". European diseases and slave raids almost destroyed these native Indian populations.

The natives speak eight different languages, but share similar religious beliefs, superstitions, feasts and ceremonies. There are four main linguistic groups in Brazil. They are the Tupi, Macro-Ge, Carib and Arawakan. All four groups are represented in the Xingu River Basin. The Kalapalo and the Kuikuro speak the Carib language.

Continues.

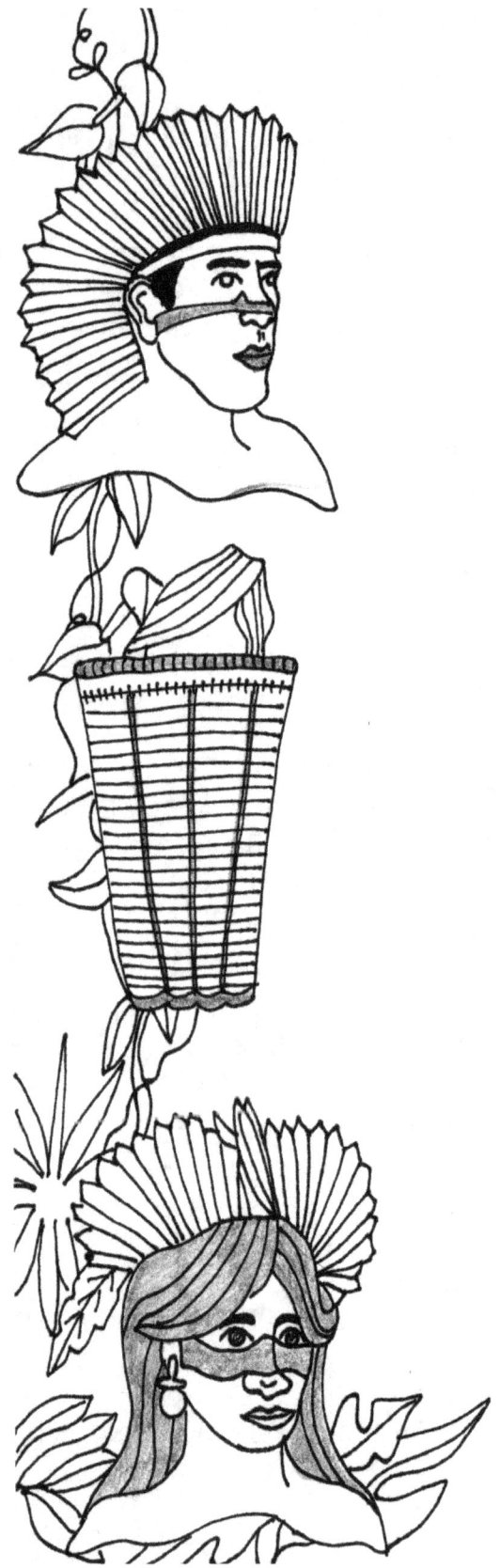

These Indians still remain in one place and practice agriculture and fishing. They grow manioc, corn, yams, potatoes and cotton. Villages are adapted to their environment, spacious, and built on solid foundations.

The houses are quite large, with roofs of straw. Each long house has two doors, each on opposite sides of the dwelling, and is built around an extensive common area. The houses are occupied by unit families rather than groups of relatives. Hammocks are hung around the outer walls leaving the central space free. Each household has a chief or head who leads family activities.

Their diet is mostly manioc and fish with scales. Only three species of birds are consumed – the curassow, jocobins and guan. They watch monkeys to determine which wild fruits are not poisonous.

The Xingu Indians share similar traditions. Each member of the tribe is free and independent to act for himself. The force of culture and tradition joins him to the tribe. A person learns skills at a young age, to behave as an adult and to seek his/her position in the community. They are very knowledgeable by age twelve.

Young boys and girls enter seclusion at about age twelve. Marriage is usually arranged and the boy is older than the girl. Xingu women usually have a shorter lifespan than men.

Most natives seem to be happy. They enjoy joking and laughing. The men and women even move from house to house dancing and singing about the latest gossip. They poke fun at fellow villagers or admonish others to follow ideal behavior.

Make an Indian Mask

The native Indians of Brazil painted their faces and wore headdresses for ceremonies. Make a mask that combines them.

MATERIALS

Sturdy paper plate (white)   paintbrush
Glue or stapler   scissors
Red, Brown and Black paint   yarn
Construction paper – red, yellow, blue, green

STEPS:

1. Cut across the plate to remove the bottom one third

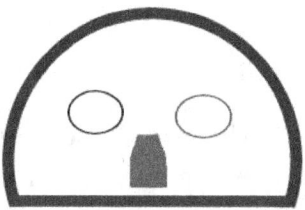

2. Draw eyes and a nose holes. Cut eye holes larger than your eyes. Cut nose as a flap (leave the top side attached).

3. Paint the face brown.

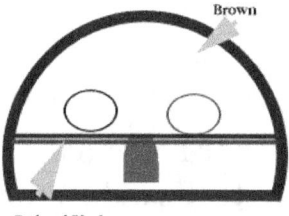

4. Using red and black paint, add a stripe across the bottom of the face which crosses the nose.

5. Cut feathers from one or more colors of construction paper (draw on them if you wish).

6. Attach feathers around the mask using glue or stapler.

7. Make holes on the side of the plate. Thread a piece of yarn through the holes and tie each in place.

Indian Tooth Necklace

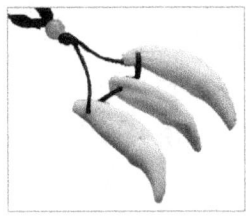

The native Indians of Brazil made necklaces using shells or teeth of animals. These necklaces were worn proudly by men or women. Create your own tooth necklace to wear with your mask or as you tell your Kalapalo story.

MATERIALS

2 cups flour	mixing bowl
1 cup salt	white or light yellow acrylic paint
1 cup water	sturdy thread and a needle
Round toothpick	baking pan

STEPS:

1. Mix flour and salt in bowl. Add water a little at a time and mix with your hands.

2. Knead dough until it is smooth and firm like clay

3. Make ½ -1" balls. Roll each ball on the table to make a long tooth shape. **The top must be thick and end must be small.*

4. Push a round toothpick through the side of the tooth and out the other side to make a hole.

5. Place teeth on baking pan and <u>with adult help</u>, bake at 325°F for about 15 minutes.

6. <u>Have an adult</u> remove them from the oven. Let them cool

7. If you want to change the color, paint the teeth white or light yellow. Let them dry.

8. Cut thread 2-3 inches longer than you want the necklace. String the teeth on thread and tie the ends of the thread in a double knot.

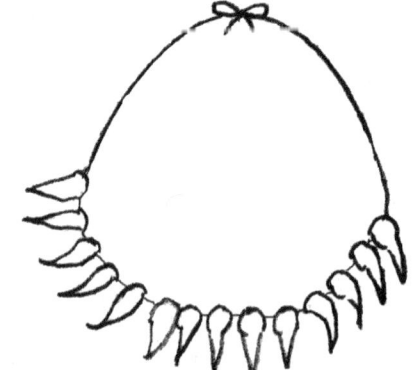

Kalapalo Stories

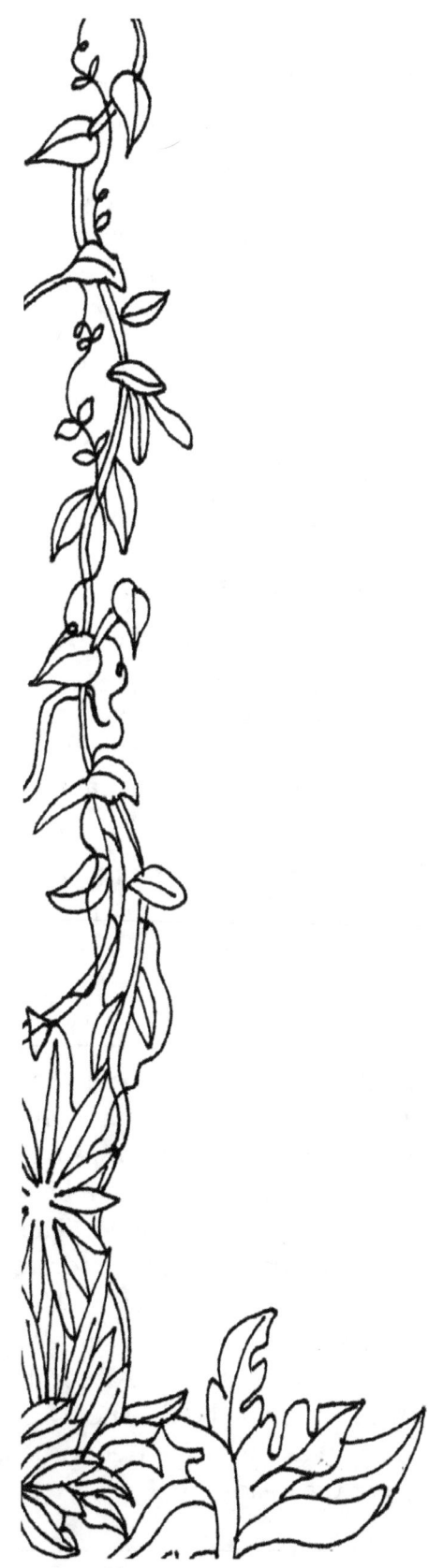

The stories of the Kalapalo Indians are organized historical narratives. They include personal accounts, myths, legend and stories of powerful beings. Many are fantasies and dreams. The stories develop over many tellings and are adjusted to the audience by the storyteller.

Kalapalo children begin listening to stories when they are young. Only the oldest leaders (*anetau*) are recognized as ones who know the detailed stories. Stories are gifts to listeners and show hospitality to visitors. Stories include events from mythological times (*ingila*) and the distant past when communities were formed.

Stories are often told at night, after the evening meal. Listeners relax in hammocks or sit near the storyteller. The stories take listeners to mysterious, beautiful settings or teach a lesson. Older people may take weeks to tell complicated histories or recall trips to special places. The storytellers use creative speech and voice changes for characters, to help the listeners see and feel the story.

The tales begin with "Do listen . . ." and end with "That's all there is to that." Storytellers begin with a loud voice and soften it as they continue talking. Active listening is expected. Listeners repeat what is heard and ask questions. Fifty to eighty percent of the stories contain quoted speech, even if the character is alone. Listeners say "eh he" or "eh he kingi" if they agree and "afiti" or "afiti kingi" if they disagree with what is said.

The characters "sleep for several days" to introduce new action. The storyteller gives the movements of the sun, seasonal changes and tells if it is night or day. The bow-masters are the warriors in the stories. Animals, plants and humans are believed to have spirits and these spirits interact in response to life situations.

Animism

The native Indians of the Amazon rainforest believe in <u>animism</u>. It is one of man's oldest beliefs. They believe all living things have a spirit – animals, plants and humans.

Primitive man probably arrived at this belief to explain the causes of sleep, dreams and death. There was a need to give a reason for the pictures some saw when they slept. The spirits were man's early explanations.

Some spirits are good and others are evil. They believe the evil spirits help cause disease. The person who leads ceremonial dances, songs and chants to these spirits is the <u>fuati</u> (*shaman*). He is the spiritual healer and can ask the spirits to help people.

The natives have many myths and legends about animism. One describes <u>Ciapora</u>, the protector of animals. He appears as a handsome young boy. He is kind, but mischievous. He walks with his feet backward to trick hunters. Some say he rides a peccary (wild hog). If the hunter thinks Caipora is near, he may create a wall of smoke to keep him away.

<u>Anhanga</u> is an Amazon goblin. He becomes angry when a hunter kills young animals. He infects the hunter with a terrible fever that drives him insane.

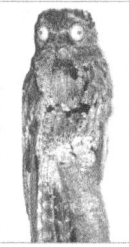
Another legend is about the <u>potoo</u>. It is a nocturnal bird with a strange, mournful cry. It is thought to be a bad omen. But long ago, the potoo had the most beautiful song in the forest.

One day the potoo fell in love with the full moon. It flew to the highest branch of the tallest tree in the forest to serenade his new love. He heard no answer from the moon, but kept flying up and up. It became exhausted and came crashing back to earth.

Hitting the ground knocked the bird half senseless. When his head cleared, he tried to recover his voice. But his voice was no longer beautiful. It was now an eerie scream and can be heard mostly on moonlit nights.

(The potoos' complex patterns of gray, black, and brown plumage resemble tree bark and his huge eyes are for spotting insects in the dark.)

According to the Indians of the Xingu, the first humans were made from logs. The Creator blew tobacco smoke over them. He tried to bring them back to life after their deaths but failed. The irreversibility of death is commemorated with the ceremony called <u>Kuarup</u>. The trunks of wooden logs serve as symbols of the dead. They are painted, decorated with feathers and male belts. The villagers keep wake over the tree trunks and weep for the dead.

The Legend of Manioc

Long ago, the daughter of the village chieftain was sent out of the village because she was pregnant. Her relatives continued to give her food as she lived in an old hut. She gave birth to a very white baby boy and she named him Mani.

When news of this remarkable child reached the chieftain, his heart softened. He restored her to her position in the village. Little Mani was a special child and beloved by all.

But one day, Mani suddenly died. He had shown no symptoms of illness. His mother buried him close to her house and spent days crying over his grave.

Eventually, she saw the first shoots of a little plant growing out of the grave. The villagers gathered around to see this unknown plant. It had strong white roots in the shape of a horn.

The people ate a small piece of the plant and said it was good. They named it <u>mandioca</u> or <u>manioc</u>. The last part of the name means horn-shaped.

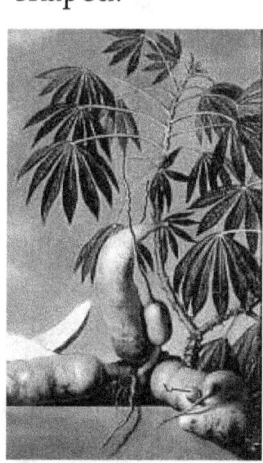

This is how we received the plant that gives life to the people who live near the Amazon River.

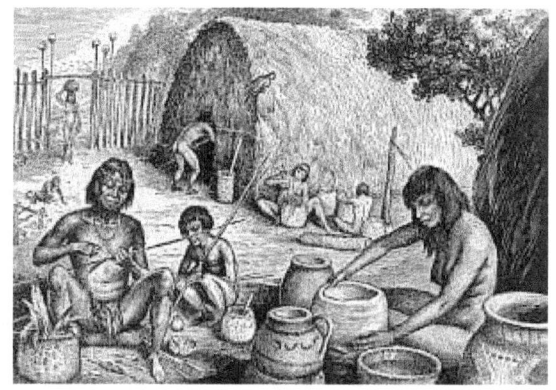

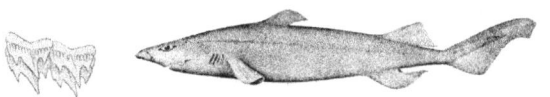

Dogfish and their teeth (used for scraping)

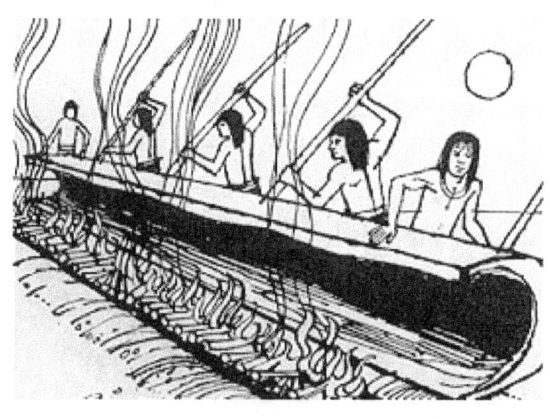

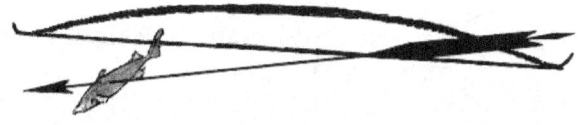

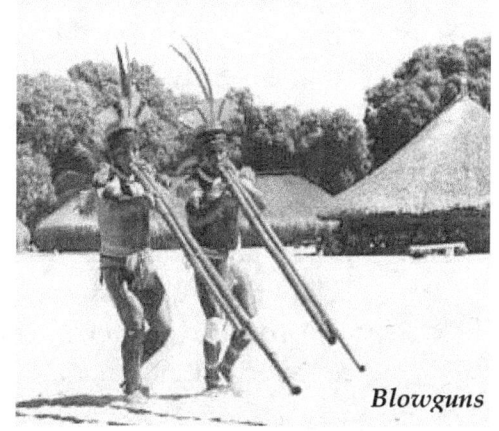

Blowguns

Photos above from free online guide on www.erroluys.com.

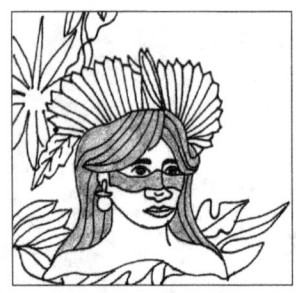

Write and Tell a Kalapalo Story

Using the information from "Kalapalo Stories", "Animism",
"The Legend of Manioc" and the list below to help you, write
your own Kalapalo story:

1. What kind of story it is?
personal narrative	historical narrative
legend	myth

2. Who are the characters?
children	shaman (fuati)
men	warriors
women	spirits
animals	enemies
plants	gods
powerful beings	monsters

3. How did they travel?
by foot	in a dream
in a canoe	a magical flight
in the form of an animal	

4. Where and when did it take place?
in the future	in the distant past
in mythological times	in the realm of powerful beings
a fishing trip	honey gathering in the forest
a trip to another settlement	at a ceremony
by a waterfall	in the plaza
home of a large snake or other animal	
on a lake, river or other watery place	
along a path or at a bathing place	

5. What important event occurred?
    left village for forest
    went through heavy rain
    approached powerful beings
    entered unknown, dangerous world

Animals of the Amazon Rainforest

The layers of the rainforest are home to more than half of the world's animals and many of them live nowhere else. There are all types and sizes. Some are colorful and others are very strange. Here are some facts you may not know about some of them:

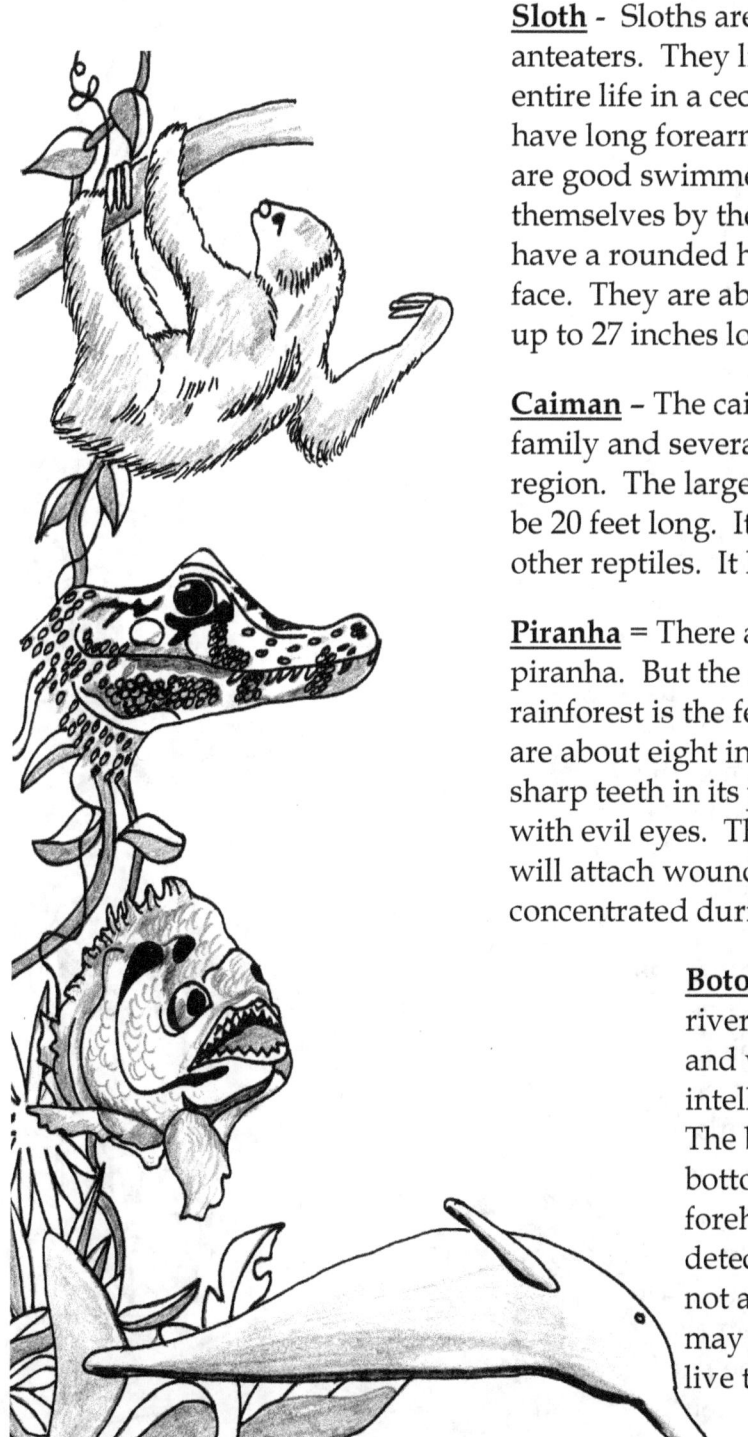

Sloth - Sloths are primitive mammals related to anteaters. They live in trees and many spend their entire life in a cecropia tree and eat its leaves. They have long forearms and long curved claws. Sloths are good swimmers, but cannot walk. They drag themselves by their claws and climb slowly. Sloths have a rounded head, small ears, and a flattened face. They are about the size of a large house cat – up to 27 inches long.

Caiman – The caiman is a member of the alligator family and several species are found in the Amazon region. The largest is the black caiman which can be 20 feet long. It eats fish, birds, mammals and other reptiles. It has a special taste for piranhas!

Piranha = There are about two dozen species of piranha. But the most famous fish of the Amazon rainforest is the ferocious red-bellied piranha. They are about eight inches long with a mouthful of sharp teeth in its jaws. The head has a short muzzle with evil eyes. They attack wounded animals and will attach wounded people. Piranhas are often concentrated during low water periods.

Boto – the boto is the Amazon pink river dolphin. It can reach 8 feet long and weight 350 pounds. They are intelligent and fearsome predators. The boto cruises slowly along the bottom eating fish. Their bulging forehead is a sonar weapon for detecting and stunning prey. Botos are not as friendly as gray dolphins and may sting with their tales. They can live to be twenty years old.

Continues.

Anaconda – The anaconda is a non-venomous constrictor and world's largest snake. It can reach 40 feet in length and weigh 550 pounds. It has very elastic jaw muscles and feeds on fish, invertebrates and small animals in bank-side shallows. It can enwrap and strangle its prey in its mighty coils. Once dead, the victim is swallowed whole. Because of its extraordinary size, the anaconda is portrayed as a monster in Amazonia.

Capybara – The capybara is the world's largest rodent. It looks like a large guinea pig and can weight up to 250 pounds! They eat riverside grass and leaves. Capybaras live in groups and are excellent swimmers. They rest in the morning, bathe in the midday and eat in the late afternoon.

Blue Morpho Butterfly – One of the most beautiful creatures of the Amazon rainforest is the blue morpho butterfly. Its wingspan is 5 ½ inches with wings of a flashy metallic blue. When it is resting, the blue doesn't show. The female has a black border round its blue wings. They pollinate plants in the forest canopy.

Green Iguana - They are the largest lizards in the Amazon rainforest. They can live high in the trees or be spotted catching sun from a tree branch that hangs low over the river. Iguanas are masters of camouflage, are excellent climbers, have good senses of hearing and smell, and unbelievable eyesight. Their long tail is spiky and sharp. They can snap it like a whip in case a predator gets too close. The tail can also break off if caught by a predator; the tail grows back. They are valuable for their meat.

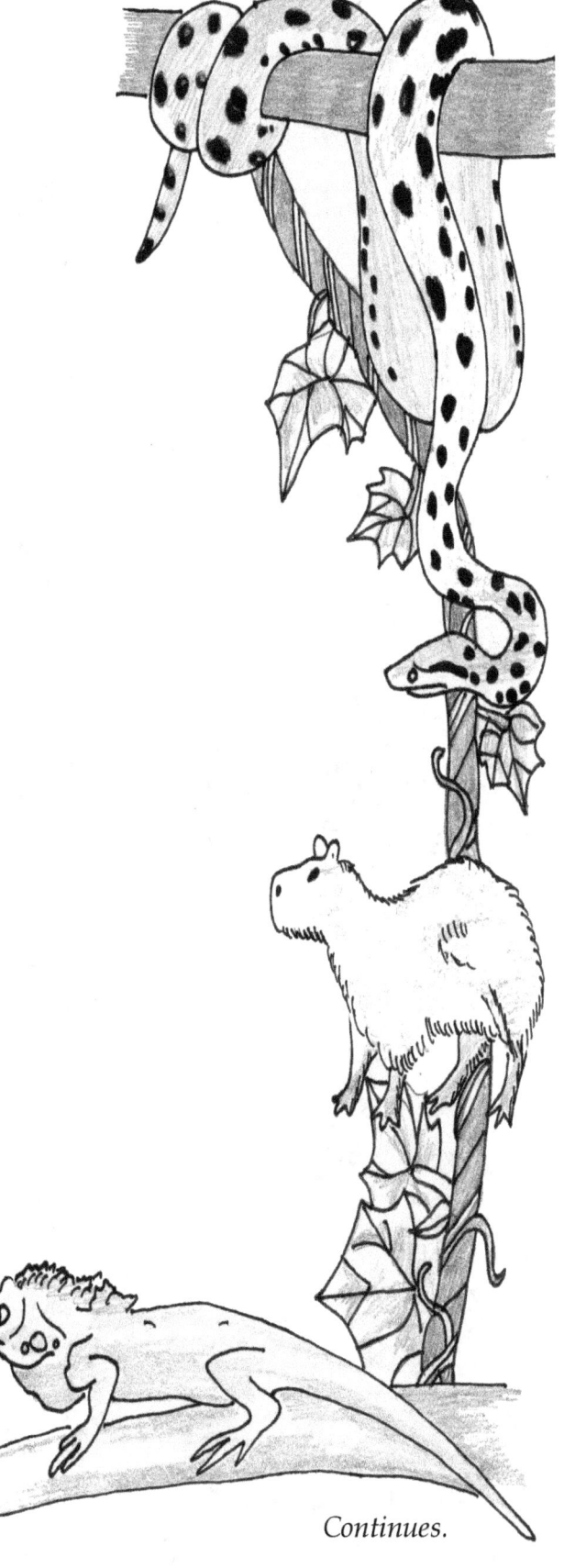

Continues.

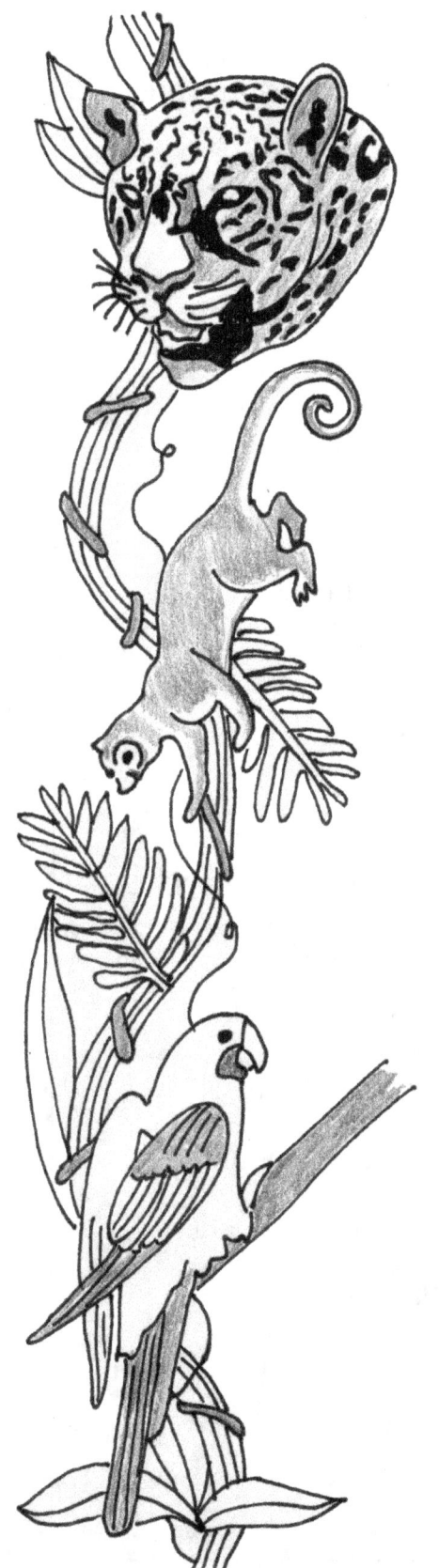

Jaguar – The jaguar is called the king of the Amazon. It is a large spotted cat that hunts near streams for deer, peccary, tapir, sloths and capybara. Jaguars can be six feet long and weight up to 250 pounds. It is usually yellowish brown but can be almost white. The lower tail is ringed with black. They are opportunistic feeders who hunt alone and seek dense cover. This powerfully built cat can also swim or climb trees for prey. The natives worship it as a god for its power and beauty (*as most pre-Colombian people up through Central America did.*).

Kinkajou – The kinkajou is a mammal related to the raccoon and coati. It looks more like a ferret or a monkey. It is seldom seen because it is nocturnal. It is hunted for its fur and meat. The outer coat of fur is gold with a gray undercoat. It has short legs and sharp claws. The kinkajou eats fruit, nectar, honey and some insects. It uses its long tail as a "fifth hand" in climbing.

Scarlet Macaw – Macaws are the largest members of the parrot family. The brilliant red feathers of this bird are used by native Indians in headdresses. It nests in hollow trunks of palm trees and eats its fruit. It has a powerful hooked beak for cracking shells of nuts and seeds. To prevent predators from finding their nests, they fly across the river to feed each morning and return at night.

Uirapuru – This charming little songbird has a melodious voice. Other birds often stop singing just to listen to it. Often called the Musical Wren, it is the subject of many legends in Amazonia. It is believed the charred remains of the little bird can melt an indifferent heart, so it is often hunted.

Continues.

Coati – The coati is a member of the raccoon family. They are about the size of a large housecat. Males can be twice as large as females. They have a slender head, small ears; and large, sharp canine teeth. Their long brown tail has rings that go all the way around and is held high. Coaties are omnivores. They eat lizards, rodents, small birds and fruit. They have a good sense of smell and skilled paws for digging.

Tapir – The tapir is a distant relative of the horse and stands about 3 feet tall at the shoulder. This brown heavy-bodied, short-legged animal can weigh up to 550 pounds. They are hunted for meat. They run in and out of steep-banked muddy streams to avoid capture. They are excellent swimmers but also move quickly over any terrain. It eats leaves, small branches and aquatic plants.

Toucan – The toucan is one of Amazonia's most spectacular and recognized birds. It has a huge brightly colored beak that can be longer than its body. It is light-weight and supported by a web of bones and tissues. The toucan uses its serrated beak like a knife to break open fruit. Its feathers are black, blue, green, brown, yellow and red.

Harpy Eagle – at 32-39 inches and a wingspan of six feet, the harpy eagle is among the world's largest eagles. It has a slate black upper side, a gray head and a white breast. This predator has huge strong legs and long, clawed talons. It makes short-burst flights from tree to tree. It eats sloths, monkeys and macaws.

Research these other fascinating animals:

giant anteater

topaz hummingbird

poison arrow frog

hoatzin

ocelot

scarlet tanager

hyacinth macaw

Amazonian manatees

umbrella bird

red howler monkey

tamandua

giant armadillo

cock-of-the rock

capuchin monkey

cotton-headed tamarin

leafcutter ant

black-tufted marmoset

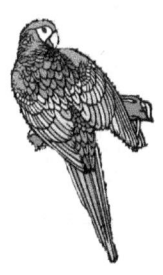

My Rainforest Animal Book

Each animal of the Amazon rainforest faces daily challenges to survive and/or thrive in this hostile environment. Choose one or more of these animals and write the story of a day in their life. Use the information in this book and/or your own research.

MATERIALS

Information about the animals   Notebook paper
White paper (9X12 inches or larger)   Crayons or colored pencils

STEPS:

1. Select animal(s) and determine the problem they will face.

2. Give your animal a name. Is he/she like the others of the species? What is special or unique about your character/animal?

3. Write a plan for your story. Include the following:

   - Describe your animal(s)

   - What is his/her problem?

   - Does he/she get any help? If so, what?

   - How does your animal/character solve the problem?

   - Is he/she successful? Why?

   - What will probably happen now?

4. Using the plan, write the story.

5. Divide the story into short sections of 1-2 sentences each.

6. Make a book using white paper. Fold or staple sheets to make pages.

7. Write a section of your story on each page beginning on the second page.

8. Write the title of your story on the first page.

9. Draw pictures on each page and color your pictures.

10. Read your story to the class or to a younger child.

Talk About the Story

1. Will Shada and Tiago marry? How did the story lead you to that decision?

2. Tiago believes the Kalapalo are good and brave. To what extent is basic character changed by events?

3. Can Tiago become the leader of his own household? Is he doing all he can to earn the respect of the Kalapalo tribe?

4. Will Papa return safely to Belém? How will his experiences in the forest change his future explorations?

5. Would you want to be fuati? Do you think Tiago will be successful in this? Why?

6. Will Tiago have problems with Kaga in the future? What could Tiago do to change Kaga's attitude toward him?

7. If you were Tiago, would you have trained to be a bow-master? If so, how successful would you expect to be?

8. Will Tiago and Hute remain friends as adults? What could split them apart?

9. Will the slave raiders come to the Kalapalo settlement? Why?

10. Describe Kambe. What characteristics will make him a good bow-master?

11. How will Grandpa respond to Tiago's decision to stay? Will he ever understand?

12. How do <u>most</u> Portuguese settlers feel about the native Indians? Could anything change their feelings? Why?

13. Will Papa ever return to the Kalapalo village? Why?

14. Why do you think the ear-piercing ceremony is important to the Kalapalo? How does it prepare a boy to be a man?

15. The Kuikuro and Kalapalo do not eat most animals? Why do you think they do this? It is a good choice?

16. Is food distribution a good tradition? When and why should it be given? Who should receive fish from a good catch?

17. How does Tiago feel about Kambe? Give <u>at least</u> three events from the story that you think prove this.

18. Will Franciscan monks come to the Kalapalo village? If they did, how would the native people respond to their teaching about God?

It Happened in Time

Each Teacher's Guide for this series of Historical Fiction has information to add to a timeline. If you made a timeline, add these events to the timeline:

TIMELINE LIST

1494 AD	Treaty of Tordesillas determined lands Spain and Portugal could claim
1497 AD	Vasco da Gama, Portuguese explorer made voyage to India
1500 AD	Pedro Alvares Cabral discovered Brazil for Portugal
1532 AD	Portuguese began shipping African slaves to Brazil
1616 AD	Portuguese fort built at Belém – an entrance to the Amazon River
* 1625 AD	**Tiago was born**
1630 AD	Portugal colonized Brazil
1638 AD	Captain Pedro Teixeira leads Portuguese expedition up the Amazon
1763 AD	Rio de Janerio becomes capital of Brazil

* Write in colored pencil

"Make Your Own" Timeline Format

<u>MATERIALS</u>

Roll of white paper 8 to 12 inches wide or sheets of white paper

Tape or glue, pencil, colored pencils

<u>STEPS</u>

A time-line should be evenly spaced. An amount of space equals a certain period of time in history.

1. Using a ruler or yardstick, make a long horizontal line beginning near the open (left) end of the paper. (If you use sheets of paper, tape or glue several sheets together to make a roll.) The line should be in the center of the paper.

2. Make a mark on the line every <u>five</u> inches.

3. Make a vertical line about <u>two</u> inches long at each mark.

4. Beginning with the first line at the left end of the paper, label each with a date. <u>Pick the first date, such as 1600 B.C.</u> The time between each line is <u>fifty</u> years, so the next one would be <u>1550 B.C.</u> Remember, years labeled B.C. are counted **backward**!

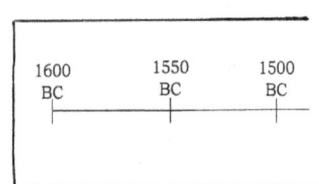

5. Label each mark until you write <u>0 B.C.</u>

6. The next line would be <u>50 A.D.</u> (Years labeled A.D. are counted **forward**.)   Label lines until you reach 2010 A.D.

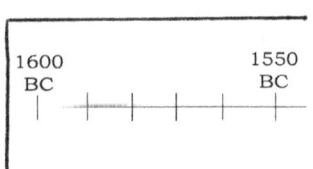

7. Return to the beginning of the time-line. Add smaller vertical lines at every inch along the line. Each space will be **ten** years.

8. Now you will add an event. Find the line for the date you want to document.   Extend the line upward. At the bottom of the new line, write the specific date. At the top of the new line write the **text**.

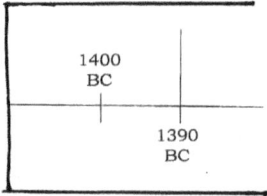

Tiago Crossword

ACROSS

1 The gourd for scraping was lined with _____ teeth.

5 Tiago's papa and Grandpa work at a _____ _____

6 A boto is a _____ _____

11 Monkey killed by Hinyu

12 Tiago's home

13 The river Tiago's family traveled on

16 King of the rainforest

17 The world's largest river

18 Main Indian food plant

20 A huge fish

21 A strong, skilled Indian warrior

22 A treasure Tiago found in a barrel

DOWN

2 Brazil is a country in _____

3 A ceremony to become a man

4 Disease mosquitoes gave Zorion

7 Friendly, helpful Indians in the story

8 Tiago joins the _____ tribe.

9 The settlers on the coast of Brazil were _____

10 Used to shoot fish

14 A lizard that runs across the water

15 Tiago's brother

19 Largest rainforest tree

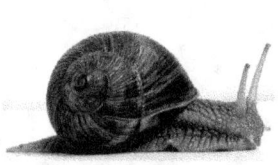
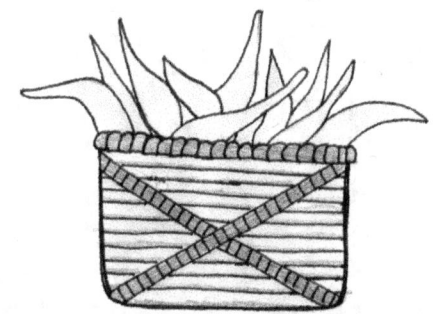
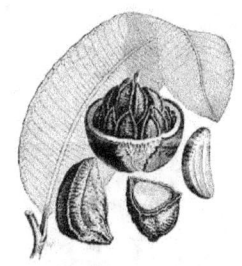

Tiago Crossword

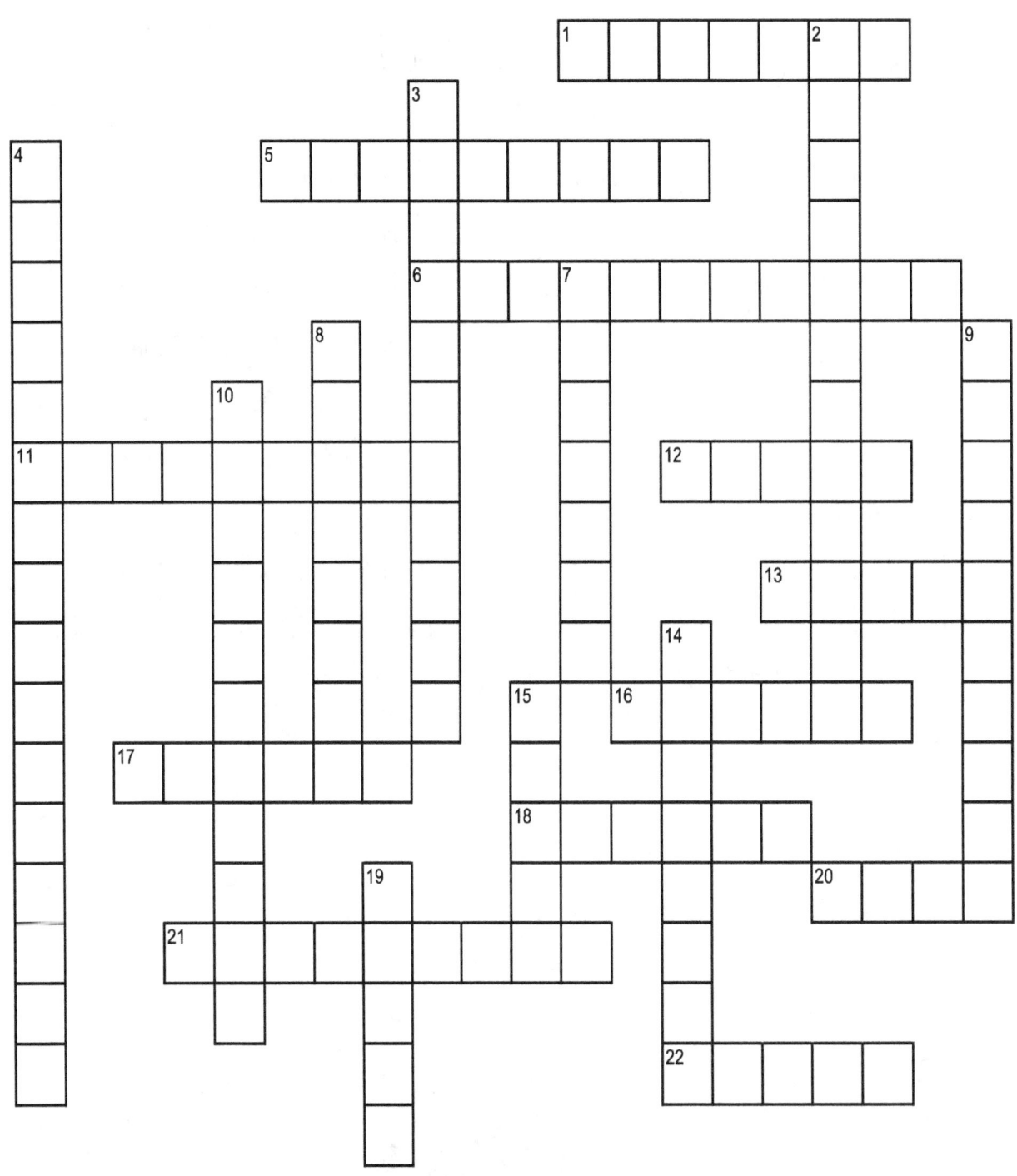

Write and Draw About the Story

1. Pretend you are a reporter. Write one of the following as an article for the Belém newspaper. Add a picture with a caption.

    Local Explorer Captured by Indians

    Eyewitness Describes a Kalapalo Ceremony

    Portuguese Explorer Marries Indian Girl

2. What do you know about the main characters from the story? Complete the Describe the Characters sheet.

3. Many Kalapalo words are introduced in the book. Using the sheet Kalapalo Vocabulary, explain the meaning of each in your own words.

4. Read the book's description of training to be a bow-master. Research the training needed to become a member of the United States Marine Corps. Complete the Bow-Master and/or Marine sheet.

5. Using the descriptions in the book, draw the Kalapalo settlement. This can be a "bird's eye view" from above or how it would be seen as you enter the front gate.

6. Research the native Indians of the United States. Compare their beliefs customs and traditions to the Indians of the Amazon.

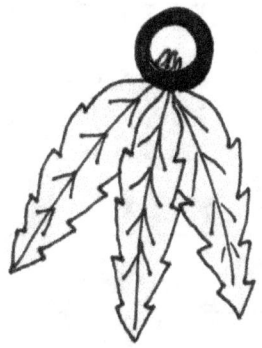

Continues.

Describe the Characters

NAME _____ DATE _____

Place a check mark in the appropriate box if the character demonstrated the trait in the story. Using the checked traits, write a description of <u>one</u> of the three characters.

	Tiago	Kambe	Zorion
Sad			
Clever			
Friendly			
Serious			
Talented			
Handsome			
Playful			
Mean			
Rough			
Kind			
Calm			
Excited			
Brave			
Strong			
Proud			
Diligent			
Loyal			

Kalapalo Vocabulary

NAME _____ **DATE** _____

Explain each of the following words <u>in your own words</u>. Use the story and the glossary to help you.

anetau _____

_____

_____

tafaku oto (bow-master) _____

_____

_____

ifutsu _____

_____

_____

itseke _____

_____

_____

kwigi (manioc) _____

_____

_____

Continues.

Kalapalo Vocabulary continued.

Kalapalo Vocabulary continued.

kwambi _____

_____

_____

fuati _____

_____

_____

kuakutu _____

_____

_____

seclusion _____

_____

_____

tane _____

_____

_____

plaza _____

_____

_____

Write and Draw About the Story continued.

Bow-Master and/or Marine

NAME _____ DATE _____

How is a bow-master like a U.S. Marine? How are they different?

	Kalapalo Bow-Master	U.S. Marine
How are they chosen?		
Skills needed		
Training		
Expectations		
Chances of Danger/ Death		
Length of Service		

QUESTIONS:

- What is the motto of the U.S. Marine Corps?

  _____

- What would be a good motto for the Kalapalo bow-Master?

  _____

Story Summary

NAME _____ DATE _____

This will be a summary of <u>Tiago, Explorer of Brazil</u>.
Write the ending of each sentence to complete the story summary.

a. Tiago and his family plan _____

_____

b. The first Indians they meet _____

_____

c. Tiago and Hinyu go _____

_____

d. Kambe falls _____

_____

e. When they reach the camp _____

_____

f. A rainbow _____

_____

g. The Kuikuro Indians _____

_____

h. Tiago and Kambe decide to _____

_____

i. Papa returns _____

_____

j. Tiago decides to _____

_____

Review: Do You Know?

NAME _____ DATE _____

1. Tiago sleeps in a _____.

2. Tiago's friend in the first part of the story was _____.

3. The fruit of his hometown was _____.

4. Father Giacinto was a _____.

5. Canoes are carved from _____ trees.

6. World's largest snake: _____

7. Feathers of this bird used for headdresses: _____

8. Fish that attacks wounded animals: _____

9. Evil Indians who attack with clubs: _____

10. People who eat people: _____

11. Weapon for shooting birds and monkeys: _____

12. Colorful bird with a very large bill: _____

13. Tiago lived in the town of _____ in the country of _____

14. The highly skilled Indian warrior is called a _____ - _____

15. Indian boys and girls enter _____ where they learn skills
    needed to be a man or woman.

16. A root used to make bread and soup is _____

17. The world's largest rodent is a _____

18. Tiago and Kambe saw a _____ across the river after the rain.

19. Dreams of the _____ _____ are a sign of a future bow-master.

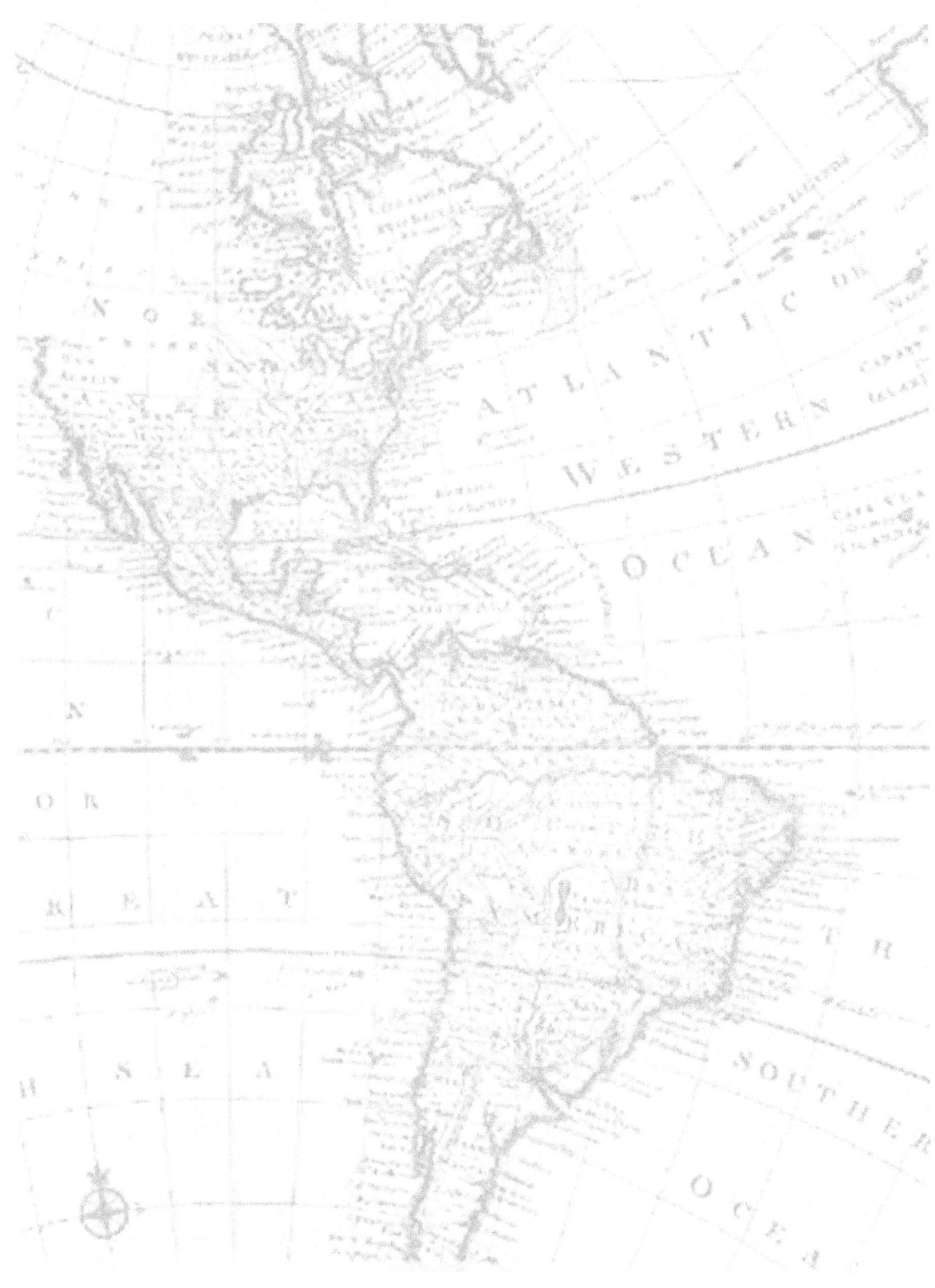

Pictures to Color

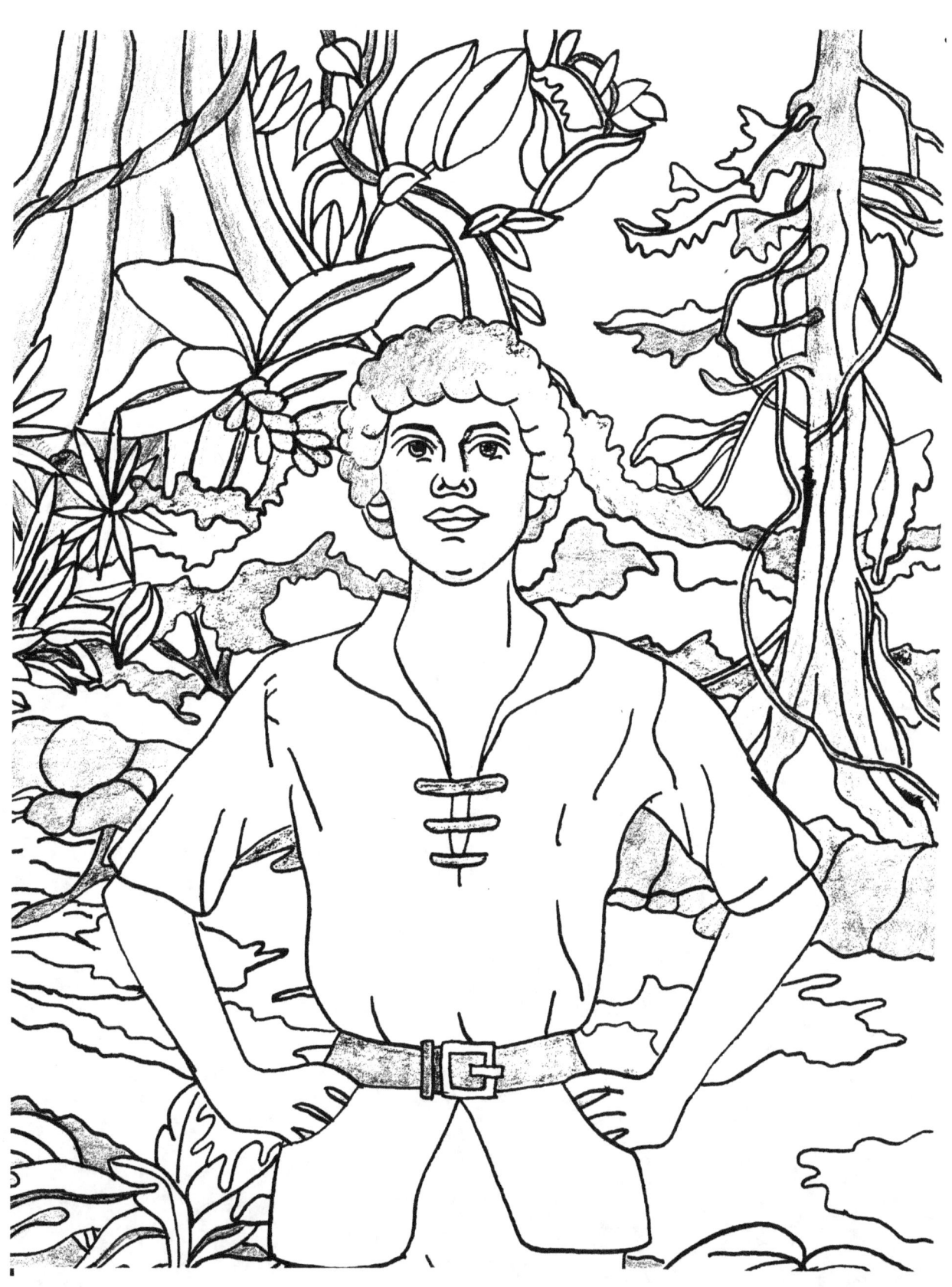

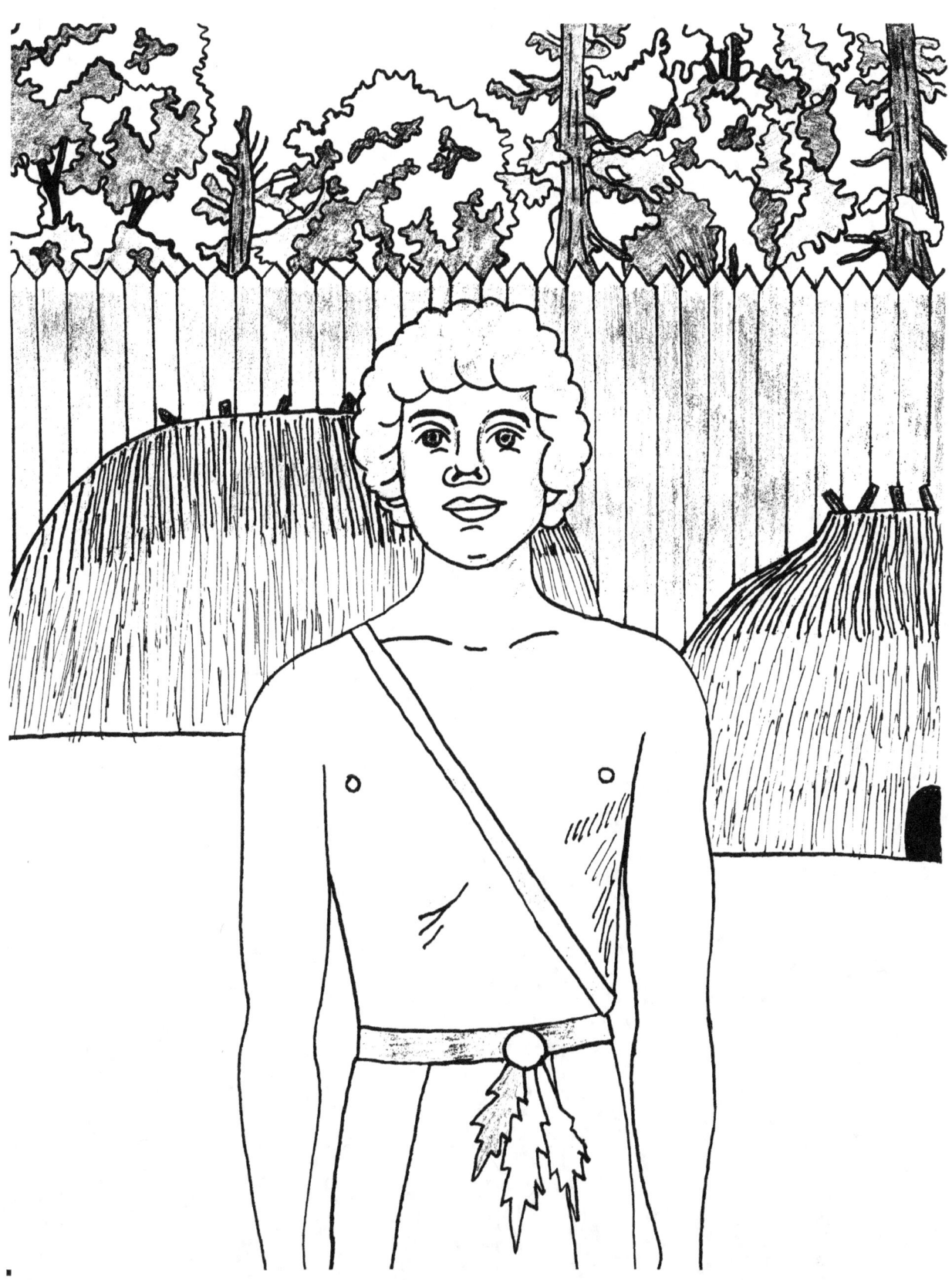

Keys and Answers

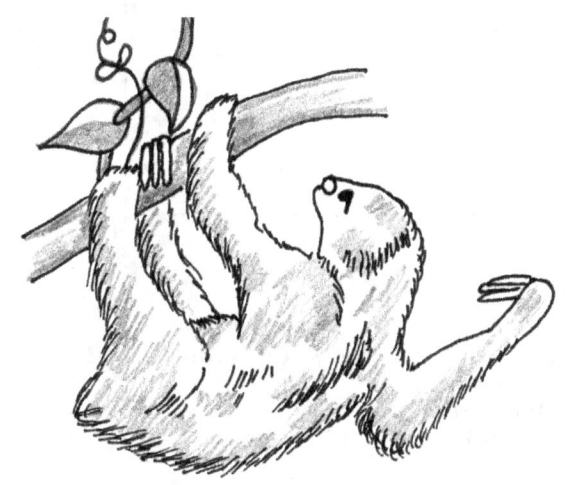

Solution to Crossword.

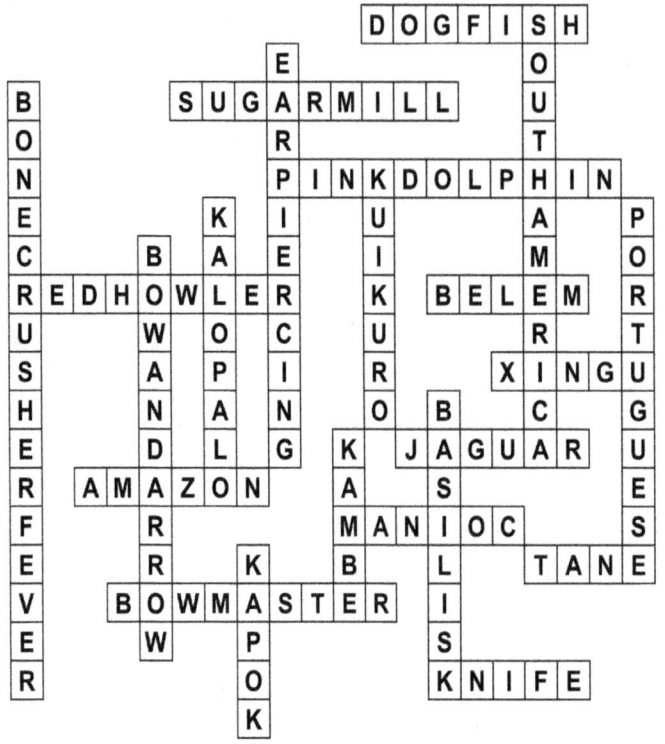

Answers:
Review: Do You Know?

1. hammock
2. Hinyu
3. mangoes
4. Franciscan monk
5. cedar
6. anaconda
7. macaw
8. piranha
9. Kayapo
10. cannibals
11. blowgun
12. toucan
13. Belem, brazil
14. bow-master
15. seclusion
16. manioc
17. capybara
18. rainbow
19. sparrow hawk

Answers: Story Summary

a. a trip up the Xingu River to the Kalapalo village.

b. are friendly. They teach Tiago to fish, teach Hinyu to kill a monkey with his blowgun and give fruit to Papa.

c. hunting and see Indians kill a peccary, wrap it up and carry it away.

d. in the river. Tiago jumps in and carries him to shore.

e. they find Mama dead and Papa and Hinyu missing.

f. a rainbow I a sign they will be protected from harm.

g. are kind and helpful. They take Tiago and Kambe to their village and to the Kalapalo village.

h. train to be bow-masters and remain with the Kalapalo

i. and is ill. Grandfather heals him. Papa leaves when he is well.

j. stay with the Kalapalo but not become a bow-master. He wants to become fuati.

Glossary

Amazon River – the largest river in the world. It begins in the Andes Mountains of Peru and flows through Brazil. It empties into the Atlantic Ocean.

anaconda – the world's largest snake, reaching 33 feet and weighing 550 pounds. It is a non-venomous constrictor that enwraps and strangles its prey

anetau – a hereditary leader and storyteller who performs rituals and songs. He has vast knowledge of traditions.

Belém – means Bethlehem in Portuguese. It is the capital and port city of the state of Para in northern Brazil. It was settled in 1616 by the Portuguese as the first European colony on the Amazon and a gateway into the interior.

bone-crusher fever (*dengue fever*) – a disease caused by mosquitoes. Symptoms are headache, muscle and joint-pain, fever and a bright red rash. This is followed by nausea, vomiting, diarrhea, a weak but rapid pulse and cold clammy skin. It can be fatal.

boto – the pink river dolphin living only in the Amazon River and its tributaries. It has tiny eyes and a humped back. It can reach age 20 or older, be eighty feet long and weigh 350 pounds.

brigantine – a sailing vessel with two masts with square sails. It carried both sails and oars for rowing

caiman – a member of the alligator family found in the Amazon region. The smallest (dwarf) caiman has yellow eyes. They are hunted for their hides.

canopy – the top layer of the rainforest where the crowns of the tallest trees are found.

capybara – the world's largest rodent; it inhabits the Amazon rainforest. It weights up to 145 pounds and eats grass and water plants.

cat's claw – a woody vine found in the tropical jungles of South America used to prevent and treat bone crusher fever.

cecropia – a tree with a gray thin trunk and leaves mostly near the top. It is a favorite home to sloths and other mammals. It is seen along riverbanks and can be 60 feet tall.

Domingo de Brieba – a Franciscan monk who traveled the Amazon River in the 1600's.

fuati – a shaman. A man who established a household, has relatives willing to live with him and who sponsors ceremonies which allow the village to help him

genipap – a tree of the tropical rainforest, 60-110 feet tall. The fruit is 3 ½ - 6 inches long and used to make a fruit wine.

ifutisu – a calm, respectful and modest nature – a trait valued by the Kalapalo

itseke – a powerful being that could cause death

jaguar – a large spotted cat called the "king of the rainforest". It is largely a solitary predator weighing up to 198 pounds. It hunts hear streams for deer, peccary and capybara.

Kalapalo – Indians of the Upper Xingu River of Brazil. They speak the Carib language. They have a strict code of ethics and do not eat land or furry animals. There are very few of them left in South America.

kapok – a majestic tree of the tropical rainforest with a smooth gray trunk and a crown of branches at the top. It grows up to 10 feet each year and may be 165 feet tall.

Kayapo – Indians of Brazil know for carrying clubs and random killings. They are physically strong and intimidate others with barely suppressed violence.

kuakutu – a house in the center of the plaza used by men to store trumpets and other ceremonial things. Men gather there to gossip and paint each other for ceremonies.

Kuikuro – Indians of the Upper Xingu River area of Brazil. They speak the Carib language.

kwambi – a dance by men dressed in ridiculous costumes and moving from house to house. They sing about gossip, witchcraft, love affairs and disputes.

manioc (*yucca or cassava*) – a shrub-like plant grown for its large tuberous roots which are used by Indians to make bread and soup. There are 20-30 varieties.

peccary – a large-tusked, wire-haired pig-like creature weighing about 80 pounds full grown

pequi – a tree of Brazil with fruit whose seeds are used for cooking oil.

piranha – the most ferocious fish in the world. There are two dozen species, but the red-bellied piranha inhabits the rivers of the Brazilian rainforest

red-howler – one of the largest monkeys in the Amazon rainforest. It is mostly red and can reach 24 inches in length. Its sound is one of the strangest in nature.

sloth – a slow-moving, medium-sized mammal of the rainforest. They eat insects, small reptiles, birds and leaves. It spends its time hanging by powerful arms and claws from cecropia trees.

tafaku oto – a bow-master, a warrior trained from an early age to be a perfectly skilled expert marksman

Xingu River (*Shin-goo*) – a large tributary of the Amazon River that flows northward for 1400 miles before emptying into the great river. The upper part (*near origin*) has many rapids.

Bibliography

Acuna, Father Cristoval de. *Expeditions into the Valley of the Amazons 1539, 1540, 1639.* London: Adamant Media Corporation, 2005.

Basso, Ellen B. *The Last Cannibals: a South American Oral History.* Austin: University of Texas Press, 1995.

Basso, Ellen B. *The Kalapalo Indians of Central Brazil.* New York: Hold, Rinehart and Winston, Inc., 1973.

Capelas, Afonso, Jr. *Amazonia: The Land, The Wildlife, The River, The People.* Toronto, Ontario: Firefly Books Ltd., 2003.

Cousteau, Jacques-Yves. *Jacques Cousteau's Amazon Journey.* New York: Harry N. Abrams, Inc., 1984.

Dalal, Anita. *Nations of the World: Brazil.* Austin, Texas: Raintree Steck-Vaughn Publishers, 2001.

Grann, David. *The Lost City of Z.* New York: Doubleday Publishing Group, 2005.

Grann, David. *Finding the Lost City: Does the jungle conceal a vanished empire?* www.boston.com. The Boston Globe, 2009.

Heckenberger, Michael J. "Amazonia 1492: Pristine Forest or Cultural Parkland." Retrieved from website: http:plaza.ufl.edu/duin/Xtra.

Kallen, Stuart A. *Life in the Amazon Rain Forest.* San Diego, CA: Lucent Books, 1999.

Lutz, Dick. *Hidden Amazon: The Greatest Voyage in Natural History.* Salem, Oregon: Dimi Press, 1999.

Page, Joseph A. *The Brazilians.* Reading, MA: Addison-Wesley Publishing Co. Inc., 1995.

Powell, Susan and Inserra, Rose. *Amazonia.* Crystal Lake, IL: Heinemann Library, 1997.

Riberio, Darcy. *The Brazilian People: The Formation and Meaning of Brazil.* Gainesville, FL: University Press of Florida, 2000.

Smith, Anthony. *Explorers of the Amazon.* London: The Penguin Group, 1990.

Wood, Michael. *Conquistadors.* Berkeley, CA: University of California Press, 2000.

http://en.wickipedia.org/wiki/Percy_Fawcett
http:/www.unmuseum.mus.pa.us/Fawcett.htm